DRAWINGS
AND
REFLECTIONS

Jeanne and Michael Spyker

AgapeDeum

Published in Australia by AgapeDeum

Contact: agapedeum.com

ISBN 978-0-6486957-1-4

Copyright © Jeanne Spyker Hardy (illustrations) 2020

Copyright © Michael J Spyker (text) 2020

All right reserved. Other than for the purpose and subject to the conditions prescribed under the *Copyright Act*, no part of this publication may be reproduced, stored in a retrieval system, or transmitted in any form or by any means, electronic, mechanical, photocopying, recording and otherwise, without prior permission of the publisher.

This edition published in 2020

Publication assistance by Immortalise
Cover illustration by Jeanne Spyker Hardy

Reflection Topics

1. A Present Jesus
2. Holy Spirit
3. Spiritual Life
4. About Grace
5. Salvation
6. Confidence
7. Ideology
8. Longsuffering
9. Awareness
10. Detachment
11. Sensing God
12. Dependence
13. Spirit Enlivened
14. Faith Renewed
15. Trust
16. God Exists
17. Spiritual Food
18. Belonging
19. Coming to Rest
20. Christmas
21. Happy New Year
22. Tolerance
23. Meekness
24. Suffering
25. God and Science
26. Burden Sharing
27. Awareness Prayer
28. Losing out
29. Religion
30. Upward Vision
31. God's Love
32. Christ in All
33. Heaven
34. Divine Support
35. Death of God
36. Easter
37. Gratefulness
38. Coming to rest
39. God's embrace
40. Rejection
41. Relationship
42. Partying
43. God in Me
44. Resilience
45. Love
46. Mental Prayer
47. Happiness
48. Faith
49. Coping
50. Intimacy
51. Sadness
52. Proximity

Reflection 1

A Present Jesus

Doors

Doors are common and found everywhere. I have walked through them thousands of times. Most doors are nothing special. Just a division between spaces. Some doors are different though. Like the front door of our home which has real significance. I tend to take little notice however, because I know it so well.

I have another important door in my life. Jesus said, 'I am the door. Anyone walking through I will look after.' Good news it is, that door. But its significance can likewise become jaded. When I lose sight of the wonderful promises that door opens into.

I must never take important doors for granted. Remain attentive and enjoy the spaces on offer. Home is a special space. As is the Jesus door that invites me into abundant living.

Reflection 2

Holy Spirit

Joint Venture

Two or more parties working together with a common goal is called a joint venture. The parties have need of each other to succeed. Success depends on good communication and performing as is expected. Then everyone will benefit.

Christians are in a joint venture with the Holy Spirit. A Senior Partner who is often perceived as rather remote and intimidating. Does the Holy Spirit actually have need of me? I have so little on offer.

God's power and perfection *does* have a need. The nature of the Holy Spirit is love and love always seeks to connect. Certainly, I have something to offer. Simply myself, and genuinely so.

In a Holy Spirit joint venture I have significance. I must play my part. Communicate with the Spirit and the partnership becomes loaded with benefits.

Divine Partnership

Reflection 3

Spiritual Life

Fluffy

Old bread is difficult to chew and swallow. A fresh loaf is nice and fluffy. Like bread, my life can dry up when circumstances come against me. Then I might develop a crust on my soul and become inflexible.

Jesus compared the workings of his kingdom with that of leaven in dough. Leaven quietly works its magic towards a fluffy loaf. But what will invigorate my life when it begins to feel stale? What makes for real kingdom living?

There are spiritual answers, like prayer. But I have discovered another one. For me the key is to remain relational when times are tough. Keep reaching out to others. I will receive back as well. And always I resist being too hard on myself. This way my soul doesn't develop a crust and life can be good.

Relationally in Tune

Reflection 4

About Grace

In the Zone

Sometimes athletes enter the zone. Everything gels together so well – it is almost otherworldly. These ultimate moments in sport may happen occasionally and make for a terrific day.

A different zone of power is that of grace. Grace is God's enablement. It becomes active by involving Jesus. Therefore, I have learned to offer brief mental prayers regularly.

Grace works in hidden ways. Awareness of this zone is particularly helpful in difficult times. And Jesus will not disappoint. Perhaps I will feel partly carried by him. Or I simply have to hang in there by faith. Either way, grace will support me.

Not that I won't lose my composure at times. Then I will shore up my spirit knowing that God's grace is sufficient for me. Grace is a zone like no other, my comfort and strength.

Divine Enablement

Reflection 5

Salvation

Banknote

Place a high value banknote money-side up on a table and you can see its worth. The church often presents salvation like that – cost side up. I am sinful and partly to blame for the price paid on the cross. But is having been born in sin my fault?

Of course not. Jesus understands me being unavoidably imperfect. I will be held responsible only when doing something wilfully wrong. Then I must owe up in prayer.

God always has that banknote face-up with the image of the Son shining brightly. The note's high cost remains flip-side down – out of sight. God sees me in Christ.

Likewise, I must see myself in Christ. My mistakes are out-of-sight. The small ones matter little; the bigger ones disappear through prayer. In Christ I am free indeed.

Spiritual Liberty

Reflection 6

Confidence

The Catch

One of our sons, when still little and standing at the top of a staircase, shouted 'Hey Dad!' Without notice he came flying into my arms down below. Now that's confidence. If only I would jump into the embrace of Jesus that readily.

Confidence is a heart matter. Our little son knew dad loved him to bits. Dad was strong and could be trusted to happily catch him.

Understanding the nature of God tells me the same. God is always close and can be depended on. Our son though could see me clearly which cannot be said of God.

Confidence involves perception and experience. Perhaps my confidence is low and needs building up. Is God really at the bottom of those stairs?

Sure thing! I must take that leap of faith and feel my confidence grow.

Leap of Faith

Reflection 7

Ideology

Stuck

Our balcony features a glass-panelled balustrade. Sometimes a bee gets up against it from the inside seeking to fly through the glass into the open space beyond. It can potentially attempt this to exhaustion. The bee needs help, over the edge into freedom. Not so a fly. It soon figures out the problem.

What is my mind like? Am I a bee or a fly? Bee-mind thinking is popular in our world. It involves ideology. Take up an idea and let it narrowly determine you. Anyone thinking differently is labelled an infidel – a deplorable.

At least the bee has the sense of being unhappy about being stuck. It sees options, but can't reach those. I prefer the fly mind, mobile and tolerant. Ideologies tend to become dictatorial, Christian ones included. Which is something Jesus never was.

An Open Mind

Reflection 8

Longsuffering

Low Range

Competent off-road vehicles have a low range option in the gearbox for climbing very steep tracks slowly. Patience and careful steering brings success. It will deliver me on top.

When in the dumps emotionally from grief, illness or a serious set-back, the same principles apply. Be patient and hold on. It needs a low range attitude. There is no quick fix, but there are possibilities. The word for this is longsuffering.

Jesus is excellent at low range. I must invite him on board and discuss things. It may not immediately solve my problems, but I will manage the path ahead and won't get stuck.

Steep tracks happen in life, which is never nice. But they offer an opportunity to appreciate the Lord better and to grow in spirit. Low range isn't altogether bad.

Spiritual Strength

Reflection 9

Awareness

Holy Leisure

Mindfulness is an old idea. In Christianity we call it holy leisure. I make sure not to become hurried and keep my mind on the present moment. Wherever I am, I have my eyes notice it properly. I taste my food with purpose, while chewing at leisure. Focussing on more than one job at a time in my thinking must be avoided. The job I'm working on is what matters. In everything I pace myself without haste.

Simple enough – and yet it's hard. Modern life insists on widespread attention. How easily can I become hurried without even noticing? I need a holy leisure day!

Quite a struggle that, but after a while it becomes easier. A day of leisurely walking with the Lord in a busy world. How good is that – for my health!

Reflection 10

Detachment

Mountain Views

It feels good when at the end of a hike you can put down your backpack, become unburdened, and enjoy a mountain view. A day of walking uphill is then well rewarded.

Everyday life is different. I tend not to unburden, but figuratively take my backpack to bed. Not ideal! Fortunately, spiritual disciplines offer a better way called 'detachment'.

Detachment begins with prayerful reflection. I hand over my problems to God and the ownership of all my belongings. I possess those by God's grace anyway. Once calm in spirit, I engage with the magnitude of Jesus and his love for me. It alters my perspective on life. Pressing matters lose their urgency. Steadily walking on in spirit, I will arrive at a mountain view and leave my backpack behind.

Reflection 11

Sensing God

Pictures

Someone looking at a picture of Amsterdam may find it simply interesting. For me, originally from Holland, a sense of that city would come flooding back. Now living in Australia those memories usually remain hidden.

Christian life can be like that. Occasionally, I may have a real sense of God. But that feeling tends to quickly fade. I don't have a picture of God to remind me either. But is that really so?

The whole of nature and humanity paints a picture of God. Its beauty and its struggles. I must remain alert to that idea – give it attention. Not that nature *is* God, but God is in nature, which holds together in God. So, I have pictures after all.

I often remind myself to notice those pictures and a sense of God becomes more real.

Spirit and Nature

Reflection 12

Dependence

Touching Base

In baseball, touch base before they tap you out and you're safe. Catch up with a special friend for a coffee and you'll touch base differently. There is a secure and good feel about getting down to base level. Something solid.

Life pulls in varied directions with sometimes unwelcome surprises. Then keeping the basics in mind helps me cope. I will seek out first base, my true friend, and know where to find it.

Jesus advised against building a life on sand. It needs a solid rock foundation against stormy weather. In my life Jesus is that foundation.

He is an ever dependable friend. When Circumstances push me about and life becomes a challenge, then I hurry towards first base. Thing is: Jesus will never tap me out there but helps me to run on.

A Solid Friend

when Tom planted the seeds
he never expected them to be
so beautiful

Reflection 13

Spirit Enlivened

Catching the Breeze

The stuff I hardly ever think about is the very stuff I cannot be without. It is so naturally available that it goes unnoticed. Until I take a dive under water. Then that stuff is quickly missed. Soon I will have to come up for *air!*

Something else in life is equally significant though just as easily ignored. It is like air, but different. Jesus said that spirit is like the wind. It is real enough, but its movements are hidden.

Not so hidden though that Christians cannot catch a spiritual breeze. In fact, it is essential that I do. I should take a deep breath of the Spirit often. Fill up my lungs with air, while telling myself that simultaneously I'm breathing in Spirit. And you know something? I'm certain that I am.

A Breath of Fresh Spirit

Reflection 14

Faith Renewed

Face Value

Older people will tell you with a smile on their wrinkled faces that they may look old but don't feel that way. Better not to take their appearances at face value. As is so readily done.

Perceiving an older person's youthfulness involves a similar process to entering the treasures of the Jesus when those seem dated. Perhaps once I believed easily, but my convictions have aged. The Gospel feels no longer vibrant.

I must refuse to take these feelings at face value. Christ within me is as youthful as ever even when the wrinkles on my soul are not. I must look past those into the inner light. My soul is not old but eternal.

I can refresh the early joys of faith by remembering them in prayer with confidence. The Lord will smooth out my wrinkles.

Soul Care

Reflection 15

Trust

Stormy Weather

When the wind blows hard and the rain pours down the place to be is home. There I can comfortably see the weather out. But how about a storm of circumstances battering my soul and drenching my spirit – what to do then?

Jesus said, 'In the world you will have troubles, but I have overcome the world.' Those words are an invitation. When troubled in spirit Jesus offers me a special place of protection. One that helps in confronting whatever is against me.

I readily accept that reality. Figuratively, I carry a second home with me wherever I go. Like a snail with a shell on its back. I do withdraw in there spiritually and become empowered by grace. From that place I stick my head out and face whatever confronts me. Rain or shine.

My Hiding Place

Reflection 16

God Exists

Pudding

Surely, you would have met someone who said that God doesn't exist. That person may insist that God's existence cannot be proven. Intellectually, that is true. A failsafe, purely reasoned explanation of God being real is impossible. Or, vice versa, that God cannot be real.

Consider a pudding. It may look unappealing. Someone may conclude that it is not a nice pudding. This conclusion is based on reason – what a nice pudding would look like. But the proof of the pudding is in the eating. Reason is immaterial to that. The pudding may well taste terrific once you take a bite.

So with God. Reason will come up short. Belief that God is real is based on a sense of God. If someone decides against that, so what. They just don't know about God like I do.

Reason's Limitations

Reflection 17

Spiritual Food

Healthy

Eat your fruit and veg today. Drink two litres of water. Buy your vitamins and do exercises. Health is big business - the modern person's success story.

My body needs looking after. But so does my spirit. I cannot live completely well by bread alone, Jesus said. Have I done some spiritual reading and reflecting today? Did I say a prayer? Has my spirit been fed?

Without eating I will soon feel hungry. My stomach will complain. When my spirit becomes undernourished, it cries out far less quickly. But the day of reckoning is ahead.

Feeling spiritually flat is neither pleasant nor necessary. A little spiritual reading, some talking with Jesus every day, plus keeping in mind that I am essentially a spiritual person, will keep me vibrant. And, of course, I must look after keep my body also.

Total Wellness

Reflection 18

Belonging

Jigsaw

Ever found a used jigsaw puzzle with a wrong piece included? It may look right, but doesn't fit. The picture rejects the piece which is left on its own. Nothing to be done about it.

In the jigsaw of relationships such a situation is the worst thing that can happen to people. When feeling not to belong within the picture of others. This lack of belonging has significant wellbeing consequences. I cannot myself create a sense of belonging. It is given to me by others.

This is serious business. Therefore, I should purposefully decide to become a placemaker. Make sure to offer significant others a sense of belonging – a place. Accept them and show real interest. Placemaking will cost me and is never easy. But it is an important Christian attitude and will do enormous good.

Opening my Heart

Reflection 19

Coming to Rest

The Jesus Prayer

A brief prayer from way back is, 'Lord Jesus Christ, Son of God, have mercy on me a sinner.' It's called the Jesus Prayer. Sinner is not meant to make me feel guilty but accepts the fact that I live under the influences of sin, also still as a Christian, and need help. I am not perfect, yet.

It is a mental prayer to be repeated in my mind. With some practice it will begin to roll on quite freely and replaces my casual thoughts with something meaningful. Also, when troubled, I can counteract it with the Jesus Prayer.

For the prayer to flow spontaneously takes time. Often I forget about it. Not so, when my mind and spirit need to settle. Then the prayer hooks effortlessly into the reality of Christ.

Effective Mental Prayer

Reflection 20

Christmas

Caterpillar

Grandpa gave Daisy and young Liam a caterpillar for Christmas. In a glass bowl with some sand and fresh green twigs. Keep an eye on it, he said. It's just like us.

The caterpillar seemed happy and ate a lot. Over time it began to spin a cocoon and disappeared. Liam and Daisy wondered about the point of it. They got up one morning and found a beautiful butterfly inside the bowl. It was amazing. They phoned grandpa all exited, who seemed happy about it too. Just like us, he said. You'll understand one day.

One Christmas, years later, Daisy remembered that gift. When Liam came visiting she asked whether he remembered as well. Oh yes, he said. The babe at Christmas is the first caterpillar. Now we all can be butterflies – in heaven. Clever grandpa, Daisy thought.

Merry Christmas.

My Metamorphosis

Reflection 21

Happy New Year

All Things New

The word 'new' tells me that '*déjà vu*' is ahead. Nothing remains new. It becomes '*seen-before*' or '*seen-no-more.*' Time and deterioration will march on. New turns into old and further expressions of the new find reality. This rhythm of life colours all. But why be that philosophical about it?

Well, this all-pervasive pattern by which everything dates and disappears has been broken. I'd best be aware of that. When Jesus said, 'I will make all things new,' he used the word in a different way. Suddenly, it was reaching beyond time and deterioration – into the 'new and never old' reality of heaven.

How about this for a New Year's resolution? Try keeping the heavenly meaning of new in mind every day. All of nature and the good you come across, you will see again forever.

Forever Young

Reflection 22

Tolerance

Sunny-side Up

With sunny-side up the yoke remains runny. Once-over and the egg becomes firm. A good childhood is like sunny-side up. Over time, it becomes flipped and my soul solidifies. In our world I need a mind of my own. I become rather inflexible.

But must the sunny-side of childhood be lost altogether? Apostle Paul suggests a renewing of my mind. Mostly that is understood as holiness thinking. But there is more to it. The renewal includes a liberation from defensive thought processes in which I am pitted against society. I must become less hardened —soften up.

Jesus desires to set me free from cynicism into tolerance. From seeing the world as a mess into knowing God to be mysteriously at work towards a great ending. That kind of thinking brings the sunny-side back into my soul.

A Happy Disposition

Reflection 23

Meekness

Know-alls

Know-alls are opinionated, bad listeners and quickly stop people from getting a word in. They are excessively confident with everything sorted. Know-alls are certain how life is best lived – for everyone. The problem is: they are wrong.

But what is the best approach to living in our world? Is there a basic quality that brings success? Real success – not what society suggests success is like. Jesus said, you are blessed when you are meek and so will inherit the earth. In other words: a humble and teachable attitude that is embracing rather than abrasive will pay off in spades over time.

Not to say that I shouldn't be my own person. Very much so. But it's how I am that person that matters. Being meek is a strength with a sure potential. It enlarges my spirit.

Attitudinal Value

Reflection 24

Suffering

Fresh Growth

As an average gardener I have learned one thing: trim a bush down well every year before spring and it will bring fresh growth. The cutting back stimulates the root system. The bush seems to notice that it needs to react positively.

Spiritual growth is little different. Most of it occurs through circumstances that peck me back. There is some suffering involved. I then have a choice whether to opt out of responding well or knuckle down in my spirit. It is never easy.

When life is doing a gardening job on me, good can come out of it. The Lord is my helper. Will I suck up strength from my roots – take a deep spiritual breath? If I do, my spirit will be adorned with fresh growth. I will become a better person.

Ever Onward

Reflection 25

God and Science

Soap Bubbles

A soap bubble drifting into the air is a fine sight. Then 'pop,' and the bubble simply disappears. People consider life to be like that – a fairly brief existence that disintegrates into nothingness. Many scientists support that view. They conveniently reject the spiritual. It is considered illusionary. No proof is offered to confirm that though.

The solely scientific outlook on life I find depressing. Is all of creation to just pop away into annihilation? Why not *believe* for better? The sciences themselves believe. They are awash with imagination. In quantum, mathematical predictions are made that cannot ever be proven as physical reality. But that's okay?

Science is to be admired. However, it will not burst my bubble. I have every right to believe that creation awaits a great eternal future. In fact, I'm convinced of it.

Scientific Limitations

Reflection 26

Burden Sharing

Merry-go-round

Life can be a merry-go-round. With running about in circles being anything but merry. It is a sorry business that is often inescapable. So how do I best deal with situations that toss me about? Can I stop the spin?

Psalm 55 advises to cast my burdens upon the Lord. Jesus will sustain me. He will strengthen my spirit and make me stand firm. It promises not that Jesus magically will change my circumstances. He may, occasionally, but usually the struggle is mine. I accept that.

Rather, the Lord's presence is a powerful dynamic within me that helps me cope. It changes perspectives. Things appear less burdensome when Jesus becomes involved. My spirit builds up resilience. My mind becomes firm. All is not that bad. I will be able to add some merry to my sorry.

Reflection 27

Awareness Prayer

Tulip Fields

In spring, as a boy in Holland, our parents took us visiting the tulip fields. Bright colours everywhere but no smell. Tulips don't emit a scent. Imagine all that beauty without fragrance.

In Solomon 2:1 the beloved calls himself the Rose of Sharon. We don't know which flower is referred to. Probably a small plant in the deserts of Israel. Just like Jesus - a fine flower in a barren land.

There have been many tulip fields in my life, so to speak. Those experiences that add colour to my days. Activities I enjoy and those that are necessary and make me feel right. But unless I keep the Lord in mind a certain fragrance seems to be lacking.

When I remember the Rose of Sharon every day, my tulip fields come up like roses.

Perfumed Living

Reflection 28

Losing out

Ice-cream

When little Jenny dropped her ice-cream on the pavement, mummy had to mightily console her. In that grieving moment Jenny was offered another ice-cream – tomorrow. Not that it helped much in her sense of loss. No more ice-cream today, that was the problem. Mummy's comforting was little noticed and tears were flowing. Would tomorrow ever come?

When I face a situation of loss, the pain is unescapable. And yet, Jesus calls that experience blessed. 'Those who mourn, shall be comforted.' God is very present in such moments. I'd best be open to that awareness.

God knows personally about grief felt regarding the state our world is in. There is plenty to mourn about. But a new and much better world awaits, one day. Like ice-cream forever! Knowing that is a real blessing. It's a certainty!

Mourning into Dancing

follow your dreams to wherever they take you...

Reflection 29

Religion

Islands

John Donne wrote years ago, 'No man is an island.' In short: we need each other. But deep down, when all falls away, I feel on my own and vulnerable. I quickly move on from this sense as best I can. That's normal.

There is no arguing with the feeling. This experience of being human has brought religion about. People feeling vulnerable before unseen spiritual realities. Modern people no longer acknowledge these insecurities however and declare religious beliefs old hat. They accept a need of each other, but have no need of God. Spiritually, they prefer living on an island – away from religion.

But the spiritual realm is for real. And I may connect with this greater reality. There are no benefits in spiritual isolation. Not when Jesus offers to be my Friend.

The Blindness of Modernity

Reflection 30

Upward Vision

Caravan

Recently, while visiting a camping show, I was humming a song written by our son Jens. 'Caravan, heading down the road.' Australia is large and camping is popular. 'I'm looking forward to the sky and I won't turn back,' is another song-line. There's actually a fine bit of Christian wisdom in that.

Christians are on a journey with ideally one eye on the road and the other on the sky. But life is full of potholes, obstacles and slippery stretches. It tends to focus both my eyes on the road and I lose the necessary perspective.

I must look up, particularly then – with confidence rather than desperation. My Helper resides in the sky and yet is always near. Like a spiritual version of satnav. Him I follow, and I won't turn back. No need to.

A Dual Perspective

Life hasn't always been easy
for Doris and Stanley
but they always look on
the bright side of life

Reflection 31

God's Love

Bathing

With a shower water bashes against my body and invigorates. My skin tingles from the liquid jets that stimulate blood flow. Sweat and grime are washed away. It's nice.

Being renewed in a bath is quite different. Relaxed and lazy I let the warm water soothe my skin. Its cleansing power is like a presence rather than an action. My soul rests in a comfortable embrace. Shower and bath – both enliven me.

God's love is like that. It's like a shower and a bath simultaneously. Love is active and stirs into action. God's love enables me towards acts of caring and being available. Love is also passive and envelops. God's love sustains me even when I'm little aware of it.

God's love is a helping presence that brings a glow into my life.

Cleaned-up for Living

Reflection 32

Christ in All

Brainwashed

Brainwashing is a mind altering process. It manipulates and seeks to align a person's perspective with that of another. The teachings of Christ however always support personal autonomy. Jesus never indoctrinates.

I was looking at the birds, the treetops, the sea beyond, and thought, 'All this exists in Christ.' That's what Scripture teaches and the mystics confirm. Not having their experiences I wondered how such an idea could become real to me. It seemed to need a gullible mind.

Still, I couldn't ignore the thought. I felt no pressure, nothing like being brainwashed. But I perceived that I should become spirit-washed, have my mind renewed by the Holy Spirit.

Now I solidly know that all *does* exist in Christ. It's not an illusion. Nature and I belong together finding our origin in the same divine Person.

Relational Vision

Reflection 33

Heaven

Pearly Gates

'No Pearly Gates,' Apostle Peter said with a smile. 'But I like to enter Heaven,' I told him. 'You are in Heaven. Almost everyone is welcome here by God's grace.' True, I had arrived in an exquisite place beyond anything ever imagined. Full of love and peace.

'I'm a Christian,' I explained. 'Yes,' Peter replied. 'You have been fortunate to know Jesus by faith alone and done okay. You're welcome – no questions asked.'

'How about a reward,' I ventured, having read about that. Immediately I felt silly about the question. Peter seemed amused. 'Perhaps. Don't ask me. And why care – really?' Yes indeed, why care, in a place like this.

'So, no Pearly Gates,' I said. 'Gates keep people out or in,' Peter explained. 'In God's realm of love there are no gates.'

Free Indeed!

Reflection 34

Divine Support

Shoulders

The idea of having a shoulder to lean on is easily understood. But I cannot lean on my own shoulders and thus need another person. Unfortunately, shoulders to lean on can be in short supply. I may not know of someone suitable. Perhaps there is a spiritual answer.

That depends on what my spirituality is like. Eastern religions offer no shoulders to lean on nor does the modern trend of mindfulness. When the chips are down, I'm on my own. The Realm beyond remains beyond.

Not so with Christianity. It offers a massive shoulder to lean on and his name is Jesus. The support of Christ is real and a very present help in trouble. It offers a spiritual type of leaning that infuses strength and comfort. Believe and you will find – the best shoulder. Readily!

Shouldering Up

Reflection 35

The Death of God

Deep Waters

A person being a deep water refers to disposition. It suggests evasiveness and unpredictability. Different from common conjugality and friendship. Better be careful.

But everyone is a deep water, though few would give that much attention. Our modern world is predominantly cognitive; deeper motivations are conveniently ignored. Thus the idea that 'God is dead' can be promoted as a rational truth. But how exclusively rational is it? Might there be an unacknowledged dynamic in play?

There always is. The rational is influenced by 'deep waters.' The human spirit is a reservoir of experiential data that affects thinking. All knowledge in essence remains a personal opinion. Possibly affirmed by others, but still personal.

I hold that God is not dead and have every reasonable right in doing so. My spirit tells me. My mind agrees.

Limits of Rationality

Reflection 36

Easter

Streets of Gold

A stranger visited the local pub telling of a place where streets are paved with gold. He declared it outside the grocery store as well. The villagers decided him to be a nice fellow with too much imagination. Mary, eight years old, excitedly told grandmother about it. Imagine walking on gold!

'You obviously believe the man,' grandmother said. 'Well, so do I.' She explained, that people these days refuse to believe in anything that makes no sense to them. It takes all the mystery out of life, which is dead wrong. Plenty is true that merely thinking cannot fathom. Something inside makes you to believe in it.

The Gospel proclaims that Jesus has risen. The power of sin has been defeated. It defies common sense, but faith tells me it is true. Happy Easter!

The Sense in Nonsense

Reflection 37

Gratefulness

G'day

G'day is a greeting well-known in Australia. It wishes you a good day, with the word good almost swallowed into disappearance. Like life in general. The bad is quickly noticed while the good often tends to be ignored. Even though circumstances may not be that bad. Many good things do happen.

With my Christian outlook on life this habit of accentuating the negative is best avoided. Irritating and troublesome situations will surely come along. I must deal with those both emotionally and practically. Then not losing sight of the good that's around is a great help.

Whatever my day, I thank God for the positives in my life and never take it for granted. This habit of gratefulness is a powerful weapon against adversity. G'day then becomes: 'Good Day!'

Overcoming Adversity

Reflection 38

Coming to Rest

Traveling Light

Cheap flights in Australia allow for 7kg free luggage. I have to select carefully when packing. Traveling light has advantages. Just cabin baggage and nothing heavy to carry.

Jesus said, 'Come to me when heavily laden and I will give rest for your soul.' This includes taking a load of my mind. My mental baggage is heavy with history – positive and negative. I must scrutinize for needless burdens. Discard what weighs me down.

For instance: I refuse to feel guilty about ordinary mistakes. I may slip up at times. But if not badly, so what? I mean well. Negative self-talk will not remain in my mental bag either.

Freedom in Christ weighs 7 kg and is packed with positive stuff. I'm loved and accepted. I keep my mind upbeat and nimble. I travel light with Jesus.

Mental Message Filtering

Reflection 39

God's Embrace

Thou-I

The concept of 'I-Thou' by Martin Buber is quite well-known. It refers to moments of experience when I sense the deep existential connection between me and another with sparkling clarity. That other may be a person, an animal, or a tree perhaps. I understand that everything originates from One Source. All is interconnected, I included. These experiences are rare.

Why do mention it? Well, I used to approach God in an 'I-Thou' manner. Struggling 'I' reaching out to a majestic 'Thou.' Until I understood having it back to front. The right way in addressing God is 'Thou-I'. God first, with little me in waiting.

It makes a difference. I simply let the 'Thou' embrace me. Then perhaps I share my concerns, which God knows about anyway. So much nicer. So much better!

ONE on One

Reflection 40

Rejection

Unwanted

In Australia we have The Reject Shop and Aussie Disposals supposedly selling items that producers have discarded – that now are discounted. This one sentence contains four words suggesting inferior quality: reject, disposal, discarded and discounted. If you thought the shops to be unpopular, think again. People like their bargains.

Our world discounts readily and that includes the value of people. Everyone has experienced rejection and knows how difficult those feelings are to deal with. They undermine wellbeing.

People may fail me, but not so the Lord. He doesn't do discounts. Only full value is considered and I'm highly prized. I need not ever feel diminishes in God's presence. I may keep my head up high. Yes, I have my imperfections. But they count for little. There is no rejection in the kingdom of heaven.

Chin Up!

rescue me from my paint pot!

Reflection 41

Relationships

Veggies

Vegetables are good for you. They bring health. Those personally grown seem to taste best. Perhaps because I have put a lot of work into them. Preparing the garden bed, keeping the weeds and pests away. I can't make the sun to shine, but will water when it doesn't rain. When I look after those veggies, they in turn look after me.

If left unattended my garden will grow wild. No effort – bad return. It reminds of my marriage to Jeanne. As with vegetables, I must care about her needs before mine. Jeanne does likewise towards me. We have agreed on that and when conflicted, it is discussed.

Vegetables take time to grow as does a good relationship. Attending well to the process makes all the difference. Love and care make the apple shine!

Reflection 42

Partying

Vanity Fair

Vanity Fair symbolises fun and enjoyment without much meaning. Superficial bells and whistles. In the story *Pilgrim's Progress* the Vanity Fair party never ends. I like having fun – but forever?

The word vanity reminds of façade. It dresses up while lacking depth. 'The Preacher' (in Ecclesiastes) concluded that most things in life are not that significant. All is vanity, he wrote. There's nothing new under the sun – whatever lives, will die and be soon forgotten. Talking about pessimistic!

But in being negative he highlighted what is *not* vanity. A few things are really worthwhile. Attend to God; attend to your partner and to your role in life. In short: be positively relational. And make sure to have a good party at times with family and friends. That is significant as well. Suits me!

Reflection 43

God in Me

Double Vision

Looking at the world with double vision is confusing. Usually it soon clears up with everything back in focus. Whatever brought on the distortion, it has been remedied.

There is an interesting idea about God's presence in my life. How far away is God really? I have life by the Spirit of God in whom our universe exists. All is made in Christ, who is not kept at a distance. However amazing, God's Spirit is personally present in all.

Richard Rohr writes, that God dwells in me as me. I like that idea. It means that God is intimate and looks through my eyes just as I do. Whatever I see and experience, I do so in and with God. That simply is, how it is. I enjoy permanent double vision – but without confusion.

Spiritual Awareness

Reflection 44

Resilience

The Bounce

When a baseball or cricket ball gets thrown to the ground it will drop there with a 'thud'. Throw a basketball or netball and it bounces back because of its flexibility. When circumstances throw me about, what will I be like?

I must bounce back. But that's not always easy. Human psychology is tricky and unpredictable. So is physical wellbeing. And what about my spiritual strength? So much to deal with – none of it simple.

I have an approach when in trouble. Never fret for that's unhelpful. Nor stay immobile, incapable of a response. Rather, remain flexible and consult Jesus about how to best react. His life is full of relevant insights.

By God's grace I'll do my best and continue learning. It keeps the 'thud' out of my life and a healthy bounce in it.

Remaining Upbeat

Reflection 45

Love

Timeless

Time just is. I can feel its reality, but what time involves exactly nobody can explain. Two other forces likewise are a mystery. The one is love and the other sin. I may sense their reality, but lack understanding of their magnitude.

Three forces that exist independently of me. If ever I give that any thought my ideas are pretty basic. Like: time rolls on, love is good and sin is evil. These forces are fundamental to God's creation though.

Of the three, love is primary. Its true reality is beyond imagination. God *is* love and God creates *in* love. Love holds our universe together. And love is to remain. Not so sin and time. One day, all of creation will reside exclusively in love's timeless embrace. A renewed and eternal creation. Jesus made that possible!

Fundamental Understanding

Reflection 46

Mental Prayer

Unseen Friend

Some children talk to an imaginary friend. That friend has a name and is real to the child. Adults look on amused. Obviously the child will grow out of such play.

Adults have *real* friends to think about. Those friends are well-known and their actuality is a given. Not so with purely internet friends. They have not been met but are trusted to be real.

Is the idea of an imaginary friend best left to child's play? Not so for a Christian. Unless I become like a child, I cannot see the kingdom of God, Jesus said. With God, childlikeness is a valued approach.

I have an unseen friend to converse with every day. A *real* friend and his name is Jesus. We delight in each other. Childlike imagination and faith complement each other.

Divine Conversations

Reflection 47

Happiness

Flowers

Put a bulb into the ground, care for it attentively, and over time it will offer itself as a beautiful flower. There is happiness to gain from such beauty when taking a moment to enjoy it. Society is fixated with happiness and for good reason. It blesses the soul.

Unfortunately, I cannot just flick a switch and become happy. I may decide to spoil myself hoping for happiness, but it tends to offer a shallow experience – more like contentment. Rather, happiness results from giving of myself non-egotistically to 'the other'. The resulting positive outcomes will make me happy. Particularly when happiness is not the primary aim of my involvement. Like cultivating flowers because they need it.

Sow well and you will reap well – but perhaps not always. Genuine happiness, or joy, is the by-product of well-intended living.

The Good Life

Reflection 48

Faith

Mirrors

Have you ever looked at a picture that is out of focus? So frustrating! Particularly, when you remember the place but cannot recognise it much. It's like looking into a mirror dimly. Which is how Apostle Paul describes our view of God's reality.

At times God has seemed unquestionably real to me. But such memories fade over time. I discern less clearly and my spirit feels less alive. It's a common problem in Christian living. If only the mirror in my soul would sharpen up.

God uses that dull mirror positively. For believing in divine reality is a matter of stubborn faith. A simple insistence that what I saw once clearly has not itself blurred at all. Only my perception of it has. Out of focus is okay, while dull-edged faith is not. I must believe!

Reflection 49

Coping

Taking a Dive

The sea is flat and shiny. Then a squall blows through with much needed rain. Waves rise up into white capped turmoil. The rain is good for my garden at home. Wind brings it along.

A calm and sunny life is always best. But having to lean into the wind at times teaches me to cope. When the breeze of circumstances becomes unavoidable and my emotions are properly soaked. With a windblown head I will then try to remain calm at heart.

The aim is to descend into my deeper spirit like a sea diver who is unfazed by the waves above. To enter into some calm and tone down my emotions, leaving whirling thoughts at bay. Mentally, I say 'stop' to thoughts and focus on Jesus. He calms the storm and is my peace.

A Regular Heartbeat

Reflection 50

Intimacy

Just to be with!

I heard a story once that made a deep impression. A little child entered the home office where father looked up from his work. 'Hi, anything the matter?' he said. The child hesitantly replied, 'No dad, I just want to be with you.' It deeply touched the father's heart.

It sums up God perfectly. Whenever I say – 'I just want to be with you' – I have fine times with the Lord. When leaving my questions and problems behind.

God knows about those, of course. But in entering the joy of the Lord such issues are best left at bay. My relationship with God must be intimate rather than trouble focused. Sure, I may mention what's bothering me briefly in closing. With serious issues I will make a petition. But really: I just want to be with the Father!

Easy Togetherness

Reflection 51

Sadness

Shadow Zone

Life is a shadow zone. A reality of white invaded by black. Sin shadows are enforcing darkness everywhere. But this darkness has been pierced by a great light. From the very beginning, when light was first called forth.

The light is Jesus. In and through him all exists. Goodness and beauty derive from his nature. Not so the shadows. And their destructive powers are increasing. An advance that saddens me.

Being world-sad, it happens. But is needs a response. As a Christian, I may yet find joy in God. Darkness should not overshadow my hope for better. I'm to focus on light rather than shadow plays. By God's grace I rise above the shadow zone.

Thus my spirit is strengthened. My hope affirmed. That one day God's light will wipe every shadow away – forever.

Silver Linings

Reflection 52

Proximity

Waiting Room

A waiting room can be a real nuisance. Particularly, when the waiting takes longer than expected. A mobile phone, magazine or book may help pass the time. I don't think anyone likes waiting rooms.

Waiting for Godot is a famous play written by Samuel Beckett. In it two friends are waiting and talking while *Godot* never arrives. The idea obviously alludes to a God who remains distant however much I expect God to appear. That suggestion is misguided. There is no room in which to wait for God's presence. God is ever present everywhere.

I may well have to wait for an answer to prayer. I may wait for moments of spiritual inspiration – for faith to stir. I may experience rich and dry times. And always God is very present. No waiting for it!

Timetable Irrelevancy

A Final Word

Hopefully you are enjoying this little book.
It is of a kind that might hang around.
For it helps in keeping spirituality fresh.
Without it taking lots of time.
Without it being tedious.

The reflections have simple but effective theology.
Of good help when taken to heart.

The pictures work their own magic.
For God relates in many ways.

As fellow travellers,
We wish you well in Jesus.

Jeanne and Michael Spyker

Books by Michael J Spyker
Available at agapedeum.com

Trilogy

Meeting Emma

A journey of discovery in which Emma becomes familiar with the many idea of Christian Spirituality through the ages. It helps her towards the person she would like to be. This book has helped many in coming to love the vast wealth of the Christians spiritual tradition.

The Primacy of Love

Jake hears about his father's ideas on God's Love from Baz while travelling the Simpson Desert. Their talks include the significance of eternal and universal love, and the relational. The story has been called a significant theological feat.

The Language of Love

Emma and Jake fall in love. JH introduces them to the real meaning of Eros well beyond merely sex. They learn about being a Friend of Jesus and the language of love. Emma and Jake set off camping in the outback in search of JH. They work out what it means to live intimately together.

Novels

Julian's Windows

A musician and a teacher of children with intellectual ability fall in love. He lost his wife. She questions her vocation as a religious sister. Country life in Victoria restores his soul. A holiday in Australia from Liverpool decides her future. The ideas of Lady Julian of Norwich are an integral part of this love story in a most natural way. Great fun and informative.

Shalomat
Jacq and Ahmed, 16 years old, are on the run through Australia on a quest with mystical dimensions. It draws them together. All seems lost but isn't quite. Young people and adults enjoy this adventure. It is partly a comment on the one-sidedness of modern society and uses ideas of spirituality and philosophy. Will there be a sequel, an appreciative reader asked?

Treatise

Science and Spirit
Science exists by the creativity of God. But where to find God within physics? Where in society, in which God has become irrelevant? An informed answer best includes knowledge of history, science, philosophy, theology and religion. Plus ideas about a way forward. A read of significance to enjoy.

Christian Living

Drawings and Reflections
52 short reflections and 16 drawings that lift the spirit. A brief story that sows an idea. A picture to enjoy. It is not so easy to stay focused in a busy world. A little help always comes in handy. There is nothing religious about this book apart from keeping Jesus in mind and living vibrantly.

www.ingramcontent.com/pod-product-compliance
Lightning Source LLC
Chambersburg PA
CBHW072019290426
44109CB00018B/2291